Sirocco
THE ROCK-STAR KAKAPO

Sarah Ell

RANDOM HOUSE
NEW ZEALAND

IT IS NINE o'clock on a wet spring night. A group of children and adults walks up a muddy path in the dark. Damp bush is all around them.

They go in a gate and gather around a small building. All that is inside are plants and logs — and a very special parrot.

HIS NAME IS SIROCCO, and he is one of only 126 kakapo alive anywhere in the world.

THIS IS HIS STORY.

SIROCCO THE KAKAPO

comes from a small island called Codfish Island/Whenua Hou, off the coast of Stewart Island, at the bottom of New Zealand. Sirocco's father is called Felix, and his mother's name is Zephyr.

CODFISH ISLAND

Almost all the kakapo in the world live on this one island. DOC moved them there to keep them safe from animal pests like cats, rats, stoats, ferrets and weasels, which eat kakapo eggs and chicks.

Codfish Island is just 14 square kilometres and is covered in thick, scrubby bush. Its Maori name, Whenua Hou, means "new land".

Anchor Island

Codfish Island

Zephyr laid two eggs in 1997, each a bit smaller than a hen's egg. Department of Conservation (DOC) rangers and volunteers kept watch over Zephyr's nest night and day to make sure she and her precious eggs were safe.

There were only 51 kakapo left in the whole world so it was a critical time. Unless more eggs were laid and more chicks grew up the kakapo was going to slowly die out.

Only two DOC rangers live full-time on Codfish Island, but other rangers and volunteers come to help them during the kakapo breeding season. Codfish Island has no roads and can be reached only by plane or helicopter.

Since 2005, some kakapo have also lived on Anchor Island in Dusky Sound, in Fiordland, and in April 2012 some birds were moved to Little Barrier Island in the Hauraki Gulf.

SIROCCO HATCHED OUT

of the egg on 23 March 1997, the day before his brother, Tiwai. Sirocco and Tiwai were tiny, weighing just 40 grams, about the size of an apricot. Zephyr fed them rich, tasty rimu berries which she had chewed up for them.

THE RIMU CONNECTION

Rimu berries

The DOC rangers checked on the chicks every few days to make sure they were healthy and growing well. They scooped the chicks out of the nest in a sieve to weigh them.

Kakapo do not breed every year, unlike most birds. Kakapo only mate and lay eggs when there is plenty of food available.

On Codfish Island, the most important food for kakapo is the fruit of the rimu tree, which ripens in large quantities only every few years. These are called mast years. On Anchor Island, kakapo also eat the fruit of the beech tree, which also has mast years.

DOC rangers keep a close eye on the development of rimu fruit on Codfish Island. They make sure female kakapo have plenty of supplementary food to eat in years when a breeding season is likely. They also offer extra food to the female birds if the rimu mast fails before it is ripe — if there is an unexpected snowfall, for example.

TIWAI WAS DOING well, but the rangers were worried about Sirocco. When he was about three weeks old, the rangers noticed that he was sneezing and his breathing sounded wheezy. They thought he might have an infection in his throat and lungs. They decided to take him from the nest and bring him into the ranger station at Sealers Bay to look after him.

Sirocco was given medicine and kept in a warm, clean environment. He was fed on a special diet of Kaytee parrot hand-rearing food. Slowly, he got stronger and healthier. At the end of the year, Sirocco was released back into the wild.

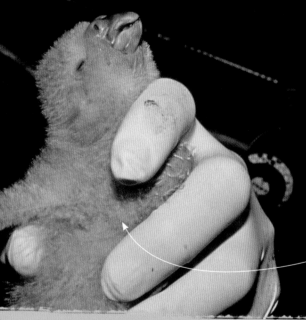

Sirocco at two weeks old. He weighed 185 grams.

Kakapo conservation pioneer Don Merton weighs Sirocco at four days old.

The rangers took in another sick young chick, called Gromit, at the same time as Sirocco. Sadly, she died when she was 80 days old. Sirocco was reared alone, away from other kakapo.

Once Sirocco could feed himself, he was allowed to live outside. He spent the first nine months of his life in a pen near the hut. The rangers spent time with him every night, talking to him and feeding him.

ONE NIGHT THE rangers were relaxing in the hut when they heard a strange noise outside. Something was scratching and scrabbling about on the deck.

They looked out into the night, and there, looking in through the glass listening to them talk, was Sirocco.

He started to do this every night, hanging around outside the hut until the rangers went to bed, before heading off to find food. It was clear that Sirocco was different to the other kakapo, who lived deep in the bush and avoided human contact.

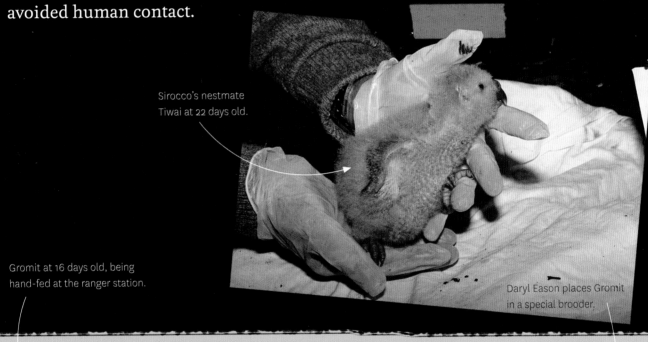

Sirocco's nestmate Tiwai at 22 days old.

Daryl Eason places Gromit in a special brooder.

Gromit at 16 days old, being hand-fed at the ranger station.

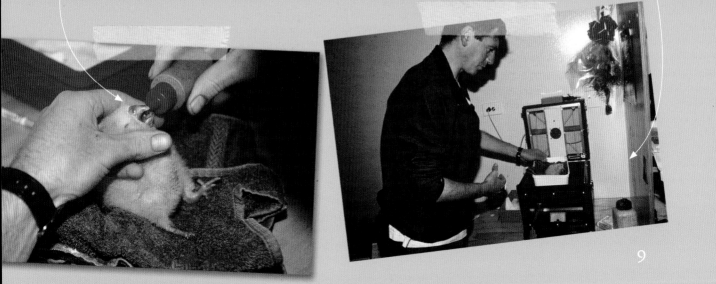

LEK BREEDING,
TRACKS AND
BOWLS

Kakapo track,
Codfish Island.

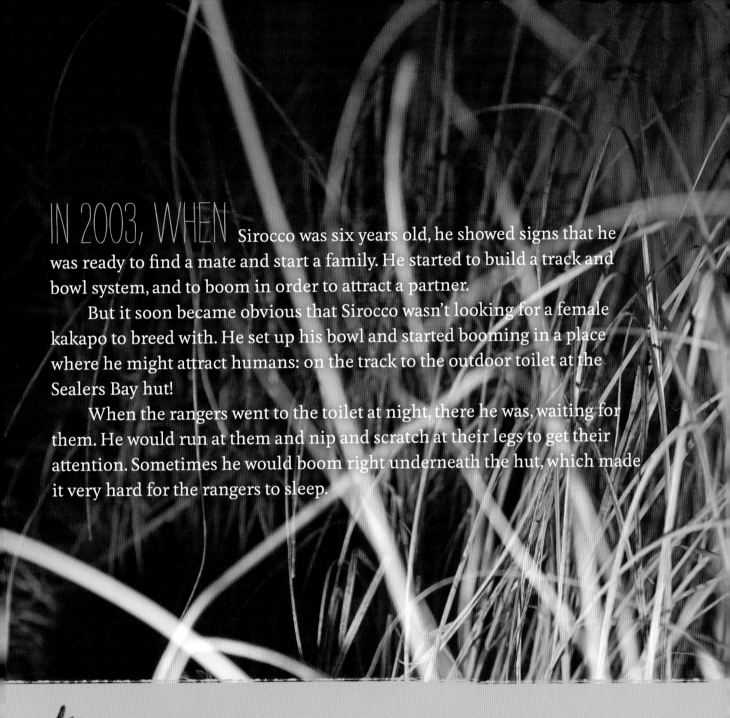

IN 2003, WHEN Sirocco was six years old, he showed signs that he was ready to find a mate and start a family. He started to build a track and bowl system, and to boom in order to attract a partner.

But it soon became obvious that Sirocco wasn't looking for a female kakapo to breed with. He set up his bowl and started booming in a place where he might attract humans: on the track to the outdoor toilet at the Sealers Bay hut!

When the rangers went to the toilet at night, there he was, waiting for them. He would run at them and nip and scratch at their legs to get their attention. Sometimes he would boom right underneath the hut, which made it very hard for the rangers to sleep.

Kakapo have a lek breeding system. This means the males put on an elaborate courtship display to attract females to mate with them. Kakapo are one of just a few species of birds in the world which act this way.

Each male kakapo creates a series of tracks through the shrubs and trees. The tracks lead to a shallow dip in the earth, which is called a bowl.

In the breeding season, from December to March, they go to their bowls each night. They inflate an air sac in their chest, blowing themselves up like a balloon. This enables them to make a sound called booming — a low, deep call which can be heard over long distances.

THE RANGERS TRIED

moving Sirocco to another part of Codfish Island, away from people, to encourage him to interact with other kakapo, but it was no use.

They tried sending him to Maud Island in the Marlborough Sounds. They hoped that he would spend time with other kakapo once he was in a different environment. But Sirocco used the opportunity to make new human friends.

On Maud, he liked to spend time with the ranger's children. One day, he was watching them jump off a wharf into the sea and decided to copy them. He waddled down the jetty and whoosh! he leapt off into the water. He then paddled ashore and shook his feathers dry. He must have been satisfied with his experiment, because he did not repeat it!

This isn't the only report of a kakapo going into the water. Rangers know kakapo can swim across small streams in the bush if they need to. But Sirocco is the only one who has jumped into the sea!

Three-year-old Sirocco being hand-fed, Codfish Island.

Kakapo chicks from the 2008 brood, Codfish Island.

Sirocco using a feeding station, Codfish Island.

13

SIROCCO'S BEHAVIOUR WAS a big problem for DOC. They needed adults to breed, but it seemed that Sirocco didn't want a kakapo family. Was there another way for Sirocco to help save his species? Could his liking of people actually be useful?

DOC BUILT A special enclosure on Ulva Island, just off Stewart Island. They fenced off an area where Sirocco could forage for food and sleep during the day, and a display pen where people could come to see him at night.

Sirocco loved being on show. Every night at dusk, he would be waiting at the door of the race which led to his display pen. He would rush down it, eager to see who had come to visit.

He liked it when people talked to him, and he especially enjoyed watching the children. He liked it when they pushed their faces up close to the glass.

SIROCCO SPENT THREE summers on display at Ulva Island. He was so popular that DOC decided to take him to Auckland, where more people could come to see him and learn about the kakapo story.

In 2009 Sirocco spent 12 days at Auckland Zoo. He was on display in the zoo's Kiwi House, and hundreds of visitors came to see him in special education and viewing sessions.

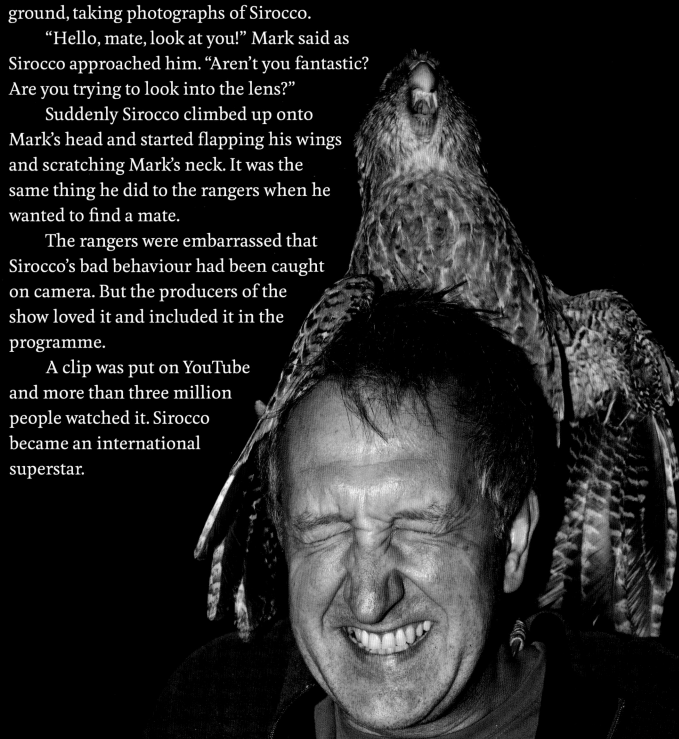

THAT SAME YEAR, Sirocco's fame spread even further. A camera crew from the British TV series *Last Chance to See* visited Sirocco and the other kakapo on Codfish Island. They were making a series on the world's rarest creatures.

The crew filmed presenter Mark Carwardine lying on the ground, taking photographs of Sirocco.

"Hello, mate, look at you!" Mark said as Sirocco approached him. "Aren't you fantastic? Are you trying to look into the lens?"

Suddenly Sirocco climbed up onto Mark's head and started flapping his wings and scratching Mark's neck. It was the same thing he did to the rangers when he wanted to find a mate.

The rangers were embarrassed that Sirocco's bad behaviour had been caught on camera. But the producers of the show loved it and included it in the programme.

A clip was put on YouTube and more than three million people watched it. Sirocco became an international superstar.

SIROCCO'S GOOD WORK

spreading the Kakapo Recovery message was officially recognised in January 2010, when he was made a conservation ambassador. Prime Minister John Key named Sirocco the "Official Spokesbird for Conservation".

"He has a worldwide fan base of people who hang on every squawk that comes out of his beak," said Mr Key. "Becoming the Spokesbird for Conservation is the natural next step."

It was official: Sirocco was famous. His nickname became

"SIROCCO THE ROCK-STAR KAKAPO".

Sirocco now has his own Facebook page and Twitter account, with thousands of followers. He also has his own website, where news about Kakapo Recovery and other conservation stories are posted.

Of course, Sirocco doesn't post updates himself — he's a bird!

DOC DECIDED TO take Sirocco on tour again in 2011, and many zoos, sanctuaries and animal parks around the country were keen for him to visit. DOC chose the Orokonui Ecosanctuary, near Dunedin, and Zealandia, at Karori in Wellington. The two sanctuaries built special outdoor enclosures just for Sirocco's visit.

Sirocco had plenty of room to sleep and forage during the day. In the evenings, he enjoyed interacting with his audience, especially when they came up close to the glass to talk to him.

Once again, Sirocco proved he was a star. All the tours to visit him were sold out, and his season at Zealandia was extended so more people could come to see him.

VERY
IMPORTANT
PARROT

This
Way
Up

kakapo

FRAGILE

Hi! I'm Sirocco.
I'm a Kakapo
Recovery ambassador

Find out more at
www.kakaporecovery.org.nz

www.kakaporecovery.org.nz

Because Sirocco is a VIP (Very Important Parrot), he gets special treatment when he goes on tour. He has a specially built travelling box with his name on the outside. He doesn't travel in the cargo area of a plane, like a cat or a dog would — he has his own seat, although he doesn't get out and sit on it.

Sirocco always travels with a 'minder'. That person's job is to look after him, make sure he has everything he needs, and talk to the public and the media on his behalf. So Sirocco really is like a rock star!

SO WHAT'S IT LIKE BEING A TRAVELLING SUPERSTAR PARROT?

When he is on tour, Sirocco spends the day sleeping, just as he does at home in the bush. Then, as it gets dark, he wakes up and starts to move around.

His minder calls to him and brings him into the display enclosure. She introduces him to his visitors and encourages them to try to get his attention. She tells the visitors all about Sirocco. People start to ask questions.

"DID THE SETTLERS USED TO EAT THEM?"
"WHAT NOISE DOES HE MAKE?"
"HOW OLD IS HE?"

His minder hands around a plastic bag containing some feathers that Sirocco has dropped, so the visitors can smell his unique scent.

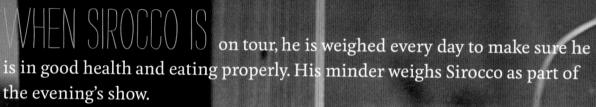

WHEN SIROCCO IS on tour, he is weighed every day to make sure he is in good health and eating properly. His minder weighs Sirocco as part of the evening's show.

In fact, Sirocco is 3.5 kilograms, about the weight of a newborn baby or twice the size of a chicken. This is a good, healthy weight for an adult male kakapo, although they can weigh as much as 4 kilograms.

Sirocco is happy to climb onto the special perch to be weighed, especially when he is rewarded with macadamia nuts or grapes.

SIROCCO'S MINDER TELLS

the story of the kakapo's decline. She talks about how the Kakapo Recovery Programme hopes to bring the species back from the brink of extinction. Sirocco's public appearances are a great help in spreading the word about how DOC staff, scientists and volunteers are working hard to keep the kakapo alive.

While his minder talks, Sirocco moves quietly about his enclosure. He walks slowly and carefully up branches and along logs. Sometimes he uses his long tail feathers to steady himself as he climbs.

Although kakapo cannot fly, they still have large wings. Sirocco flaps his wings when he is fed treats, as he would have done when he was a chick being fed by his mother.

ONCE THE SHOWS

are over, Sirocco has the rest of the night off. His minder lets him back into a large fenced area of bush at the back of the display enclosure, and he scurries off into the darkness.

She meets him at the top of the hill and gives him some special treats in a feeding box. Then it is time to say goodnight and leave him to his nightly wanderings.

As his minder walks away down the hill, Sirocco makes a loud "skraark!", the only sound he has made all evening. Is he saying "good night", "go away!" or "come back!"?

Sirocco doesn't usually like to be handled, but he appreciated being able to get out of his box when he got seasick on his way out to Maud Island.

MAUD ISLAND

WHEN HE IS not on tour, Sirocco no longer lives on Codfish Island. Because he has been all around New Zealand, he cannot go back to Codfish in case he introduces bird diseases or parasites to the other birds there. Kakapo are so rare we cannot afford for any to get sick or die!

Sirocco has a health check before going on each of his trips and when he comes back. At first, he is placed in quarantine for three weeks. Once test results are back and DOC staff are sure he is healthy, he is released back into the wild.

When Sirocco is at home, he doesn't have anything to do with humans for most of the year. He lives over the ridge from the ranger's house, and he keeps to himself. It is only in the breeding season that he seeks out humans and tries to attract their attention.

Maud Island is a closed sanctuary, so visitors have to get a special permit to land there. However, it is more accessible than Codfish Island, so Sirocco gets quite a few visitors.

Sirocco's new home is Maud Island, in the Marlborough Sounds at the top of the South Island. He is currently the only kakapo on Maud Island, but it is home to other rare birds such as the takahe and kakariki, as well as a special frog that lives only on Maud Island, and the Cook Strait giant weta.

AT THE END of 2011, an American animal trainer called Barbara Heidenreich came to visit Sirocco. She is an expert on parrots. DOC wanted her to work with Sirocco to make his time on tour more enjoyable and to stop him from bothering humans so much during the breeding season.

Sirocco was a good student. He learned quickly and seemed to enjoy the training. He soon started to obey simple instructions in exchange for treats. And because he enjoyed having something interesting to do, he became less aggressive.

SO WHAT LIES IN SIROCCO'S FUTURE?

As he is only a young bird by kakapo standards — just 15 years old — he hopefully has many years as a conservation ambassador ahead of him. DOC plans to take him on tour each year to zoos and sanctuaries around New Zealand so many more people can meet him and learn about the kakapo story.

The kakapo species is in much better shape now than when Sirocco was hatched. There are more than twice as many birds, and most of them are young ones who can make a big contribution to the breeding programme. Since 2007, 44 new chicks have hatched and been raised.

But it is not all good news for the kakapo. Recently, five birds have died — one of them, Waynebo, may have been nearly 100 years old. And in 2011-12 there was no breeding season.

Trying to bring the kakapo back from the brink of extinction is a long, slow process, and only time will tell if it is successful. In the meantime, Sirocco will do what he can to tell the world that some things — like kakapo — are too precious to be lost forever.

"No one else has kiwi, no one else has kakapo. They have been around for millions of years, if not thousands of millions of years. And once they are gone, they are gone forever. And it's up to us to make sure they never die out."

— Don Merton, conservationist, 1939–2011

The kakapo is a parrot, but it is only distantly related to other parrots, such as the cockatoo and macaw. Its closest biological relatives are the New Zealand native parrots, the kaka and the kea.

The Kakapo is the heaviest parrot in the world, and the only one which cannot fly. However, kakapo can climb trees using their large feet and strong beaks.

Kakapo have powerful legs, enabling them to walk several kilometres at a time, and to run fast if required to escape from predators.

"Me kauhi ranei koe ki te huruhuru kakapo, pu mai o te taonga?"
Shall I cover you with the feathers of the kakapo, heaped up here from the south?
— Maori proverb

The Maori name kakapo means night parrot. The first European settlers called kakapo the owl parrot, because the feathers on its face make it look like an owl.

The kakapo's Latin name is Strigops habroptilus, which comes from the Greek words for "owl" and "face", and "soft" and "feather".

The kakapo is the world's only nocturnal parrot, which means it is active mainly at night.

Like all kakapo, Sirocco always wears a VHF radio transmitter, so he can't get lost at home or on tour. DOC staff can track him easily in his enclosure, or if he escaped or was stolen. You wouldn't get far with him!

Scientists believe kakapo can live to be up to 100 years old.

DOC boosts the natural diet of the remaining kakapo with a special pellet, to keep the birds healthy and help them produce more eggs in the breeding season. During breeding, the pellets also help mother birds raise their chicks if rimu fruit is in short supply.

"[Kakapo] could be caught in the moonlight, when on the low scrub, by simply shaking the tree or bush until they tumbled on the ground, something like shaking down apples. I have seen as many as half a dozen kakapos shaken off one tutu bush this way." — Charlie 'Explorer' Douglas, writing in 1899

KAKAPO FACTS

Scientists believe that, many hundreds of thousands of years ago, the kakapo was much lighter and able to fly. But as there were no ground-dwelling mammal predators in New Zealand, the kakapo slowly lost the power of flight.

Sirocco's other nicknames are the Big Green Budgie of Love, His Highness and Sir Occo.

Sirocco has a habit of stealing the Crocs shoes belonging to the rangers and taking them back to his bowl.

Kakapo have a unique, sweet, musty smell, which has been described as being like the inside of an old violin case. It is very distinctive, which may have made kakapo easy for predators to track.

KAKAPO Q&A

WHY ARE KAKAPO SO RARE?

Before the arrival of humans in New Zealand, the only natural predator the kakapo had was a giant eagle, which is now extinct. They lived undisturbed, their mottled green feathers blending in to the colour of the bush.

Maori used to hunt kakapo for food and for their feathers, which they made into warm cloaks. But more damage was done by the rats and dogs which came to New Zealand with the Maori, and then with European settlers from the early 1800s. Rats, ferrets, weasels and stoats brought by the settlers ate the kakapo's eggs and young, and cats and dogs ate the adult birds, too.

As forest was cleared for farmland, there were fewer places for kakapo to live. The birds became more and more rare.

By the middle of last century, many people believed kakapo were extinct. Very little was known about them, and few people had ever seen one.

HOW DID KAKAPO RECOVERY START?

Conservation workers were not ready to give up on the kakapo, however. Some birds had survived in the far corners of Fiordland and Stewart Island, and expeditions in the 1960s caught a few male kakapo. Sadly, they did not survive in captivity. By 1974, kakapo experts knew of no living birds. They made a last desperate quest to find any surviving kakapo.

After much searching over several years, some birds were found in Fiordland. But they were all males. Without female birds, the kakapo was doomed.

RICHARD HENRY

Richard Henry and his dog, Lassie, which he used to capture live kakapo.

Then, in 1980, the first female kakapo seen for more than 70 years was caught on Stewart Island. Several more females were also found there. It seemed at last that there was some hope for the species.

To keep the birds safe, rangers moved them all from their natural homes in Fiordland and Stewart Island to predator-free island sanctuaries.

Recently, some trampers reported hearing kakapo booming in mainland Fiordland. Maybe some birds still survive there, in isolated valleys.

kakapo to live on a fourth island, Maud Island in the Marlborough Sounds.

WHERE DO KAKAPO LIVE NOW?

Although kakapo once lived all over New Zealand, there are now only three main populations: on Codfish Island/ Whenua Hou, off the coast of Stewart Island; on Anchor Island in Dusky Sound in Fiordland; and on Little Barrier Island in the Hauraki Gulf. Sirocco is the only

WHAT DO KAKAPO EAT?

In the wild, kakapo eat a wide range of plant foods. They are vegetarian, so eat only leaves, nuts, seeds and fruit, buds, bark and the roots of ferns. They seem to like plants which are not very tasty to other birds and often have a strong flavour. Kakapo especially like the fruit of rimu and beech trees.

When Sirocco is on tour, he eats a range of different foods. He is allowed to

One of the first people who tried to save the kakapo from vanishing was a man called Richard Henry. In the late 1800s, he pushed for special island sanctuaries, free from animal pests, to be set aside to protect native birds such as the kakapo and kiwi. He moved hundreds of birds to Resolution Island in Dusky Sound in Fiordland. Unfortunately, stoats eventually managed to swim to the island and started to kill birds.

Henry abandoned his conservation attempts in despair.

"The mother Kakapo is also quite fierce, and charges so viciously that 'Foxy' gets a fright and barks. She stands over the young ones, or between them and the danger, and has, no doubt, learned to do so to protect them from the rats . . ."

Richard Henry, writing to the Commissioner of Crown Lands, Dunedin, 1894

forage in his enclosure but is also fed the leaves of blechnum ferns, hound's tongue ferns and astelia, and supplejack vines. Grapes and macadamia nuts — special treats for kakapo — are hidden around his display enclosure to encourage him to move around.

Other treats include the cones of kauri trees, which would once have been eaten by North Island kakapo. To Sirocco these are like toffee apples!

At home on Maud Island he also eats the needles of the many pine trees that grow on the island, and the stems of tutu, a plant which is poisonous to mammals but not to kakapo.

WHAT SOUND DO KAKAPO MAKE?

Unlike other parrots, kakapo are very quiet. Sometimes at night they make a loud call which sounds like "skrark!" Scientists think they make this noise to let other kakapo know where they are. This is the only noise female kakapo make.

In the breeding season, however, male kakapo make a lot more noise. Each night they make their booming call by inflating an air sac in their chest. In between bouts of booming, they make a noise called "chinging", which is more high pitched. During the breeding season they can boom and ching all night trying to attract females. This makes Codfish Island a noisy place to try to sleep!

Because Sirocco has spent so much time with humans, he also sometimes makes a mumbling, chattering noise. DOC rangers think he is copying the sound of people talking.

HOW DID SIROCCO GET HIS NAME?

Kakapo Recovery team members give

Amateur botanist Walter Buller described the kakapo as "remarkable" in his book on the birds of New Zealand, published in 1872–73. This illustration from the book is by Joseph Keulemans.

Some early European settlers kept kakapo as pets. Governor Sir George Grey kept a kakapo as part of his private zoo at Kawau Island, north of Auckland. He described it in a letter to a friend as being more like a pet dog than a bird. In this picture, southern explorer Quinton McKinnon poses with an expedition party in 1888, including a pet kakapo.

THE KAKAPO OR OWL PARROT
STRINGOPS HABROPTILUS

every kakapo a name. Many of the birds are given Maori names, such as Awhero (meaning hope), Aranga (meaning resurrection) and Morehu (meaning survivor). Some older birds have funny names like Gumboots, Smoko and Whiskas.

Sirocco is one of several kakapo named after winds — the sirocco is a hot wind that blows off the desert in north Africa. His mother is called Zephyr, which means a gentle breeze, and her mother was named Nora, after the north wind. Three of Zephyr's other chicks were also given "wind" names.

WHAT DO KAKAPO DO DURING THE DAY?

During daylight hours, all kakapo sleep. In good weather, they will climb up to the top of a tree, like a manuka or totara, and roost on a branch, sometimes as high as 20 metres off the ground. When it is raining, they sleep in holes in the ground or in the roots of trees, or under ferns, flax or a tussock-like plant called gahnia. Some birds have favourite sites, and others will sleep anywhere.

Unlike other birds, which might live in pairs, family groups or flocks, kakapo are solitary. This means adult kakapo live alone, apart from other birds. However, scientists are not sure if this has always been the case, or if it is because there are so few kakapo left that they can each have their own space!

Introduced rats are one of the biggest threats to kakapo. Here are the remains of a kakapo chick and two eggs, attacked by rats on Codfish Island.

One of the first kakapo found in Fiordland in the 1970s was named Richard Henry, after the pioneer conservationist. Richard Henry the bird played an important part in the kakapo breeding programme and helped to save his species. He was believed to be more than 80 years old when he died in 2011. Holding him is Don Merton, a pioneer in the rescue and recovery of kakapo, who died the same year.

THE KAKAPO RECOVERY PROGRAMME — TURNING THE TIDE

The Kakapo Recovery Programme is overseen by a partnership — established in 1990 — between DOC, New Zealand Aluminium Smelters Ltd (NZAS) and conservation organisation Forest & Bird. NZAS operates the Tiwai Point aluminium smelter at Bluff.

The Recovery Programme was established around the time Sirocco was hatched, when kakapo were in serious decline. A special team of rangers and scientists was set up, and money was put towards research to find out more about kakapo and how to encourage them to breed. And it worked. By 2008 there were 91 kakapo, a 78 per cent increase in population since 1985.

Every 10 years the Kakapo Recovery Plan is updated. The current plan is to manage the kakapo population so that it continues to increase, with a minimum of 60 adult females by 2016. Another important aspect of the plan is to maintain and increase public awareness of kakapo and their need for conservation —

which is why Sirocco's work as a travelling ambassador for the Recovery Programme is so important.

Money is also put towards important research into artificial breeding, supplementary feeding and kakapo genetics, and into developing technology to track and manage birds better.

The long-term goal of the Kakapo Recovery Plan is to restore the mauri (life-force) of the kakapo species by having at least 150 adult females.

HOW CAN YOU HELP?

The most important thing you can do to help the kakapo is to spread the message, like Sirocco does. The more people who know about kakapo and care about their survival, the better.

Donations to the Kakapo Recovery Programme are gratefully received. Part of the royalties for this book will be donated to the programme.

If you are over 18, you can volunteer to work in the field with kakapo during the breeding season.

And if you are in Fiordland or Stewart Island, keep an eye out for signs there might be kakapo about. You might be lucky enough to find an undiscovered bird!

Find out more about the Kakapo Recovery Programme and its work at www.kakaporecovery.org.nz

SOURCES AND FURTHER READING

WEBSITES

www.doc.govt.nz

www.forestandbird.org.nz

www.kakaporecovery.org.nz

www.kcc.org.nz (Forest & Bird's Kiwi Conservation Club)

BOOKS

Alison Ballance, *Kakapo: Rescued from the brink of extinction*, Craig Potton, Nelson, 2010.

Buller's Birds of New Zealand: a new edition of Sir Walter Lawry Buller's 'A history of the birds of New Zealand', from the 2nd edition, 1888, Whitcoulls, Christchurch, 1967.

Mark Carwardine, *Last Chance to See: In the footsteps of Douglas Adams*, Collins, London, 2009.

Gideon Climo and Alison Ballance, *Hoki: the story of a kakapo*, Godwit, Auckland, 1997.

Rod Morris, *Kakapo*, Reed, Auckland, 2006.

Sy Montgomery, *Kakapo Rescue: Saving the world's strangest parrot*, Houghton Mifflin Books for Children, Boston, Mass., 2010.

Robin Ormerod, 'Henry, Richard Treacy — Biography', from the *Dictionary of New Zealand Biography. Te Ara — the Encyclopedia of New Zealand*, updated 1 September 2010, www.TeAra.govt.nz/en/biographies/2h30/1

ABOUT THE AUTHOR

Sarah Ell was brought up in a conservation-mad household, belonged to a junior naturalists' club and went on many Forest & Bird outings as a child. She loves the outdoors, sailing, reading and writing. She lives with her family on Auckland's North Shore, and has been lucky enough to have Sirocco nibble her hand.

ACKNOWLEDGEMENTS

Thank you very much to the helpful and committed staff of the Department of Conservation, especially Karen Arnold, Daryl Eason, Deidre Vercoe Scott and Alisha Sherriff; Ferne McKenzie; and Trish Irvine at DOC Auckland.

Thanks to photographer Rob Suisted for his fabulous images of Sirocco at Zealandia. Thanks also to Jo Moore and Zealandia, Mark Carwardine and Barbara Heidenreich and Tama Pugsley for letting us use their photographs.

Thanks to Jenny Hellen and the team at Random House; and to designer Kate Barraclough for making Sirocco's story look fantastic.

Thank you to Rob and Florian, and Florian's Nana Ruth, for keeping the household running while I wrote the book.

And, of course, thank you to Sirocco himself, a bird with incredible presence and charisma, who has such an important role to play in the future of his species.

INDEX

Anchor Island 5, 7, 41
animal pests 4, 40
Auckland Zoo 16
booming 11, 42
Carwardine, Mark 19
Codfish Island/Whenua
   Hou 4-5, 7, 12, 33, 41
Eason, Daryl 9
Felix 4
Gromit 8, 9

Heidenreich, Barbara 34
Henry, Richard 40
Kakapo Recovery
   Programme 44-45
lek breeding 10-11
Little Barrier Island 5, 41
Maud Island 12, 32-33, 42
Merton, Don 8, 37, 43
Orokonui Ecosanctuary 22
natural predators 4, 40

Richard Henry (kakapo) 43
rimu 6-7, 41
Tiwai 6, 7, 8, 9
track and bowl system
   10-11
Ulva Island 15, 16
Waynebo 36
Zealandia 22
Zephyr 4, 5, 6, 43

IMAGE CREDITS

DOC: pages 4, 5, 6, 7, 8, 9, 10 (lower), 12, 13 (lower left and right), 21 (lower left), 41, 42 (top); Tama Pugsley: page 13 (top); Mark Carwardine: pages 18 and 19; Jo Moore/Zealandia: page 22 (lower); Barbara Heidenreich: pages 32 (top), 34, 35, 44, 45; Hocken Library: page 40; Alexander Turnbull Library: page 42 (lower left); Te Papa Tongarewa: page 42 (lower right).

A RANDOM HOUSE BOOK published by Random House New Zealand
18 Poland Road, Glenfield, Auckland, New Zealand

For more information about our titles go to www.randomhouse.co.nz

A catalogue record for this book is available from the National Library of New Zealand

Random House New Zealand is part of the Random House Group
New York London Sydney Auckland Delhi Johannesburg

First published 2012

© 2012 text Sarah Ell, photography Rob Suisted, except those credited above.

ISBN 978 1 86979 831 4

Design: Kate Barraclough
Cover photographs: Rob Suisted

Printed by 1010 Printing International